God is the friend of silence. See how nature — trees, flowers, grass — grow in silence? The more we receive in silent prayer, the more we can give in our active life.

Mother Teresa

101 ways to relax and reduce stress

Candy Paull

SPIRIT  PRESS

101 Ways to Relax and Reduce Stress
ISBN: 1-40372-016-9

Published in 2006 by Spirit Press, an imprint of Dalmatian Press, LLC.
Copyright © 2006 Dalmatian Press, LLC. Franklin, Tennessee 37067.

Editor: Lila Empson
Text and Cover Design: Whisner Design Group

06 07 08 09 QSR 10 9 8 7 6 5 4 3 2 1

Printed in Canada

14934

Each of us makes
our own weather,
determines the color
of the skies in the
emotional universe
which he inhabits.

Fulton J. Sheen

Contents

Contents continued...

Introduction

When you are relaxed and calm, your energy is well focused, you can think clearly, and you are able to plan and organize your thoughts effectively. You live harmoniously in body, mind, and spirit.

101 Ways to Relax and Reduce Stress offers a combination of practical help and inspirational insight. Created to encourage you in the midst of a busy life, this book not only addresses the outward symptoms of stress and tension, but also encourages you to examine the root causes, which are often spiritual in nature.

This book will help you live a more enjoyable and peaceful life. May you be blessed as you seek to live each day in the light of God's love.

God gives us always strength
enough, and sense enough,
for everything he wants us to do.

John Ruskin

Come to me, all you who are weary and burdened, and I will give you rest.

Matthew 11:28 NIV

#1

Check Your Attitude

How you think about your life can make a difference in how you experience life. If you always focus on what you don't have and what is wrong, you will create more stress through your frustration and negativity. Choose instead to focus on what's right and good in your life. A positive mind-set helps you develop a lighter, happier attitude that cushions the bumps in the road.

Set your intention to trust God instead of dwelling on negative circumstances. A trusting attitude opens the door for positive change, just as opening a window allows fresh air to circulate through a stuffy room.

attitude

Your eyes are windows into your body. If you open your eyes wide in wonder and belief, your body fills up with light.

Matthew 6:22
THE MESSAGE

>> When you catch yourself complaining, exchange your complaints for praise and thanksgiving.

#2

Write a Personal Prayer or Affirmation

> *It shall come to pass that before they call, I will answer; and while they are still speaking, I will hear.*
>
> Isaiah 65:24 NKJV

prayer

Tap into the power of prayer. A creative way to align yourself with God's highest will for your life is to write an affirmative prayer. One way is to personalize a Scripture verse and make it into a prayer: The Lord is on my side and I am not afraid (Psalm 118:6).

Another way is to create an affirmative sentence that addresses a challenge you might be facing. Here are a few affirmations to get you started:

* My good comes to me under grace in perfect ways.
* Before I call, I am answered.
* God is my unfailing supply.
* I am divinely led.

>> Create a one-sentence personal affirmation or prayer. Write it on an index card and carry it as a daily reminder.

#3

Live in the Present Moment

Have you ever noticed how often your mind dwells on the past or in the future? You may be in the midst of a conversation with a friend, but your mind is leaping ahead to the errands you still have to complete. You may be eating a delicious lunch, yet you replay a past argument in your mind.

Choose to focus on God's presence in your life instead of worrying about the future or regretting the past. Enjoy the moment while it is here. Savor the meal you are eating. Be fully present to your friend. Be aware that every moment is a gift and a miracle.

moment

> *In the present, every day is a miracle.*
>
> James Gould Cozzens

>> Take a five-minute "life appreciation" break. Breathe deeply. Look at what's around you. Be aware of the simple wonder of here and now.

#4

Watch Your Language

Out of the abundance of the heart the mouth speaks.

Matthew 12:34 NKJV

language

What you say mirrors what you believe. Your language affects the way you perceive your life. It's easy to be unaware of the chatter that runs through your mind when you are doing other things. By becoming conscious of your thoughts, you can consciously choose words that bring you back into the presence and provision of God.

Substitute faith-filled statements for words of disbelief. Instead of saying "I can't afford," say "God is my source." Instead of saying "I can't," say "I will." When thoughts of worry fill your mind, use the power of praise as a reminder to you of God's love and care for you.

>> Notice what kinds of statements you make in your mind. Transform your limiting statements (I can't, I'm not) to freeing statements (I can, I choose).

#5

Stretch Like a Cat

Imagine a cat curled up in a ball, sleeping in the sun. Now watch that cat awaken, yawn, and stretch out with long, long legs and torso. Cats know the wisdom of stretching. God's creatures teach simple lessons through the very nature of their being.

Stretching is good for the human being, too. Stretch your body with a good yawn and a big stretch—this is an especially good idea if you've been hunched over a computer. Stretch your mind with a stimulating conversation, a challenging puzzle, or a new idea. Stretch your spirit with prayer, meditation, and spiritual reading.

stretch

We must always change, renew, rejuvenate ourselves; otherwise we harden.

Johann Wolfgang von Goethe

>> Take an exercise class that stretches your body. Read a book that stretches your mind and spirit.

#6

Wiggle Like a Worm

As obedient children, let yourselves be pulled into a way of life shaped by God's life, a life energetic and blazing with holiness.

1 Peter 1:15
THE MESSAGE

wiggle

There is nothing more wiggly than a group of children. The younger the children, the more they wiggle. When they sing "Jesus wants me for a sunbeam," their faces will shine like beaming suns. When you want to get their attention, just ask them to pretend to be something. "Fly like a butterfly! Wiggle like a worm!" The children will dance gleefully around the room, delighting in the joy of life.

When you're feeling old and jaded and tired, become like a child again. Rediscover the sheer joy of wiggling like a worm and dancing like a butterfly. Lift your arms and praise God.

>> Take off your shoes and wiggle your toes. Be like a child and move your body freely and joyfully.

#7

Take a Hike

hike

Traffic jams. Crowds and noise. Chores at home. Obligations at work. Daily life can wear down your soul and make you tired. Nature is out there waiting to renew you. Go away to where the only traffic is a deer crossing the path or a squirrel skittering up a tree. Follow a winding trail through the forest and enter a world of beauty far, far away from everyday cares and worries.

Jesus left the crowds behind and went to the wilderness to pray. Spend time away in God's creation. A walk in nature's beauty will renew your spirit.

> *I like to think of nature as an unlimited broadcasting station, through which God speaks to us every hour, if we will only tune in.*
>
> George Washington Carver

>> Take an afternoon walk in the forest. Pack a lunch and make it a day to be away from the cares of your life.

#8

Soak in the Tub

> *My body was made for the love of God. Every cell in my body is a hymn to my creator and a declaration of love.*
>
> Ernesto Cardenal

soak

When your nerves are frazzled and you're tired from a hectic workday, a soothing soak in the tub can give you a mini spa-vacation. A hot bath with essential oils or Epsom salt can ease sore muscles. A warm bath with soft scents can help you get to sleep more easily.

Write yourself a prescription for a half-hour of personal renewal. Take a long, hot soak in the tub. Let this be a time to meditate on the events of your day and to ask God's guidance for the morrow. Make your bath a time of rest and renewal.

>> Spend some time in the tub tonight. Let the pleasures of the bath soothe away your cares.

#9

Sing in the Rain

The day may be gloomy, with dark clouds and showers. Your mood might match the day. Light the fires of your heart with a chant of praise, a hymn of wonder, or even a funny doo-wop song that makes you laugh. You don't have to be a great singer to enjoy the benefits of making music.

When you sing, your whole body resonates with the sound. You take deeper breaths and get more oxygen into your system. Singing can heal your body and give your spirit a lift. Express yourself and make melody in your heart. The music will bring sunshine into your soul.

sing

> Speak to one another with psalms, hymns and spiritual songs. Sing and make music in your heart to the Lord.
>
> Ephesians 5:19 NIV

>> Sing a song or chant a psalm aloud. Sing in the shower and know that God listens with pleasure when you sing.

#10
Breathe Deeply

Breathe on me,
Breath of God, till I
am wholly thine,
till all this earthly
part of me glows with
thy fire divine.

Edwin Hatch

breathe

Babies breathe naturally and easily, filling their lungs with air and releasing their breath fully. Adults often lose that sense of ease and openness, taking more shallow breaths and restricting the inflow and outflow of breath.

Do you take quick, shallow breaths? That kind of breathing creates tension. Take a gentle, deep breath, feeling it reach down toward your belly. Exhale with an audible sigh. Did you feel your body relax as you exhaled? In the Bible, the words for *spirit* and *breath* are often interchangeable. As you notice your body's breath, remember to breathe in the love and energy of God's Spirit.

>> Lie on your back. Spend ten minutes breathing gently and deeply, allowing your breathing to relax and refresh you.

#11

Practice Mindfulness

Ease the stress in your life by focusing on what you are experiencing right now. Instead of dismissing the details of your daily life as unimportant, choose to treat everything you do—even humble household chores—as important to God.

Practicing mindfulness is a simple way to bring your attention back to what God is doing in your life right now. For example, when you wash dishes, concentrate on the act of washing dishes. Feel the silkiness of the warm water. Take pleasure in the clean dishes. Allow the Spirit to whisper to you through the simple metaphors of daily living.

practice

> *God speaks to all individuals through what happens to them moment by moment.*
>
> J. P. DeCaussade

>> Practice focusing your mind on experiencing the moment. Set aside worries, plans, regrets—and pay attention to what you are doing right now.

#12

Take Time to Smell the Roses

Never lose an opportunity of seeing anything that is beautiful, for beauty is God's handwriting—a wayside sacrament.

Ralph Waldo Emerson

smell

A dewy rose smiles at you from a neighbor's garden. Daisies dance by the roadside as you drive to work. A planter full of impatiens colors the entrance to the bank. A receptionist's desk holds a bouquet of roses and a card celebrating a special occasion. The beauty of a flower is a reminder of God's creative presence, even in the midst of a busy day.

Do you take the time to stop and smell the roses? Smell a rose. Watch a flaming crimson-and-gold sunset. Slow your hurried pace and take a moment to let the beauty remind you of the glory of creation.

>> Buy a single rose and place it in a vase on your desk at work. Let it remind you to savor the beauty of life.

#13

Eat for Energy

Forget the doughnuts and coffee. The artificial stimulants of sugar and caffeine will leave you depleted. Your body needs quality fuel to run on. Your mother was right when she told you to eat your vegetables. Raw vegetables and vegetable juices can give you long-lasting energy, and fresh fruit will give you a gentle boost of natural sugar right away. Nuts, whole grains, and lean meats give you balanced nutrition that will take you through the day.

If you've been living on fast foods and packaged snacks, try a healthier way of eating. You'll discover new energy and feel good about yourself.

energy

> *Please test your servants for ten days. Give us nothing but vegetables to eat and water to drink. Then compare our appearance with that of the young men who eat the royal food.*
>
> Daniel 1:12–13 NIV

>> Snack on fresh raw vegetables and delicious fruits instead of doughnuts, chips, and cookies. Try this for a week and see how you feel.

#14

Purify Your Body with Water

> *Whoever is thirsty,*
> *let him come; and*
> *whoever wishes, let*
> *him take the free gift*
> *of the water of life.*
>
> Revelation 22:17 NIV

purify

If you're thirsty, grab a glass of water. Water helps cleanse toxins from your system. According to scientific experts, dehydration has negative effects on your metabolism. A decrease in water consumption contributes to fatigue. Dehydration can also have a profound effect on brain function and energy level. Start the morning with a glass of water. Sip water during the day to sustain energy and mental clarity.

The Bible uses water as a metaphor for purity and life. As you cleanse your body with pure water, remember also to purify your spirit with prayer. Meditate on spiritual thirst and what the water of life means to you.

>> Drink a glass of water first thing in the morning, reminding yourself to stay pure in thought through the day.

#15

Enjoy Laughter with Friends

Have you been taking life too seriously lately? Does life seem more like an uphill climb than a romp in the meadow? If so, maybe you need a time-out with friends. Relaxing with friends puts problems in perspective. Friends are there for you through tears and laughter. As you share your troubles and triumphs, remember the grace that has brought you through this far.

Whether you're laughing at a silly joke or praying for one another, friends make life worthwhile. Ensure that love and laughter are a part of your week. Call some friends and make time for fun together.

enjoy

> *Laughter can relieve tension, soothe the pain of disappointment, and strengthen the spirit for the formidable tasks that always lie ahead.*
>
> Dwight D. Eisenhower

>> Make a date to spend some time with good friends. Do something that makes you laugh and feel good.

focus

101 ways to relax

create

choose

savor

stretch

and reduce stress

dance

walk

soak

#16

Turn Down the Media

God is the friend of silence. See how nature — trees, flowers, grass — grow in silence? The more we receive in silent prayer, the more we can give in our active life.

Mother Teresa

turn

The six o'clock news offers a litany of war, horror, corruption, greed, and trouble. The front page of the newspaper details the latest scandal. The media offer a constant flow of chatter, opinion, and advertising. Though it's important to know what's happening in the world, you also need time to listen to your spirit.

Ration your media exposure. Consider going on a media fast for a few days. Instead of watching television, spend time in prayer and meditation. Turn off the radio and let the silence soothe you. Finish a neglected project. Give yourself quiet time for communion with God.

>> Instead of listening to the radio as you drive, turn off the talk and the music and enjoy the quiet.

#17

Surround Yourself with Supportive People

The world offers plenty of negative comments and criticism. You don't need more criticism—you need encouragement and support. A circle of supportive friends can encourage you to reach your full potential and make life easier and more fun.

Think about your inner circle. Who believes in you, supports you, and has a positive attitude? Which friends drain your energy with complaints, criticisms, and a negative outlook? Pray about whom you should spend more time with and whom you should spend less time with. Actively seek to surround yourself with supportive friends.

surround

> *Encouragement is oxygen to the soul.*
> George M. Adams

>> Develop a mutual encouragement society: a circle of friends who support, encourage, and believe in one another.

#18

Put Lavender in Your Medicine Chest

> *Ointment and perfume delight the heart.*
>
> Proverbs 27:9 NKJV

soothe

Victorian ladies used it in their smelling salts. Its flowers have soothed people to sleep for centuries. You can enjoy a whole medicine chest of benefits in one small bottle of high-quality lavender essential oil. Called the "Swiss army knife" of aromatherapy, lavender is a great introduction to using essential oils for wellness.

One or two drops of lavender essential oil can calm a headache or help you release the day's stress and get to sleep at night. From soothing itchy insect bites to calming frazzled nerves, lavender eases stress on many levels.

>> Buy a bottle of high-quality lavender oil (be sure it is labeled by its botanical name, *lavandula augustifolia*) for your medicine cabinet.

#19
Take Your Vitamins

Getting the right nutrition into your body is important for dealing with stress. Eating well every day, along with finding and taking the right combination of vitamins and minerals, helps your body recover from the effects of stress more quickly.

Just as you fuel your body with vitamins, so also you need to fuel your faith with spiritual nutrients. These can include prayer, quiet time alone with God, meditation, Bible reading, and reading books about the spiritual life. Long walks also nourish the soul and help you remain strong and calm in the midst of a busy life.

vitamins

Half the spiritual difficulties that men and women suffer arise from a morbid state of health.
Henry Ward Beecher

>> Check out the vitamin section at a local health-food store. And check out the "spiritual vitamin" section in your local bookstore, too.

#20

Listen to Your Heart

May the words of my mouth and the meditation of my heart be pleasing in your sight, O LORD, my Rock and my Redeemer.

Psalm 19:14 NIV

listen

Schools teach with an emphasis on facts, figures, and quantifiable knowledge. You live in a practical society that rewards head knowledge that can be tested or applied to a utilitarian purpose. Straight-line thinking and ten easy steps to achieve goals are highly valued.

The ways of the heart are more mysterious. Your heart speaks with a wisdom that is more intuitive, connecting you with your spirit. When you are weary of the ways of a utilitarian world, take time to listen to the deeper wisdom of your heart. It will teach you about love and help you receive guidance from God.

>> In the middle of a busy day, take a moment to become still. Close your eyes, place your hands over your heart, and listen to what your heart tells you.

#21

Remember That Your Body Is God's Temple

When Paul wrote to the church in Corinth, he used a metaphor to remind them that they were a holy people in body as well as spirit. In a world of temples dedicated to many gods and goddesses, he reminded them that their physical bodies were living temples in which the Spirit of God dwells.

Remember that your body is God's temple. It is a beautiful expression of God's creativity, entrusted to you to use wisely. Honor the beauty of the human body by taking care of yourself. Honor the spiritual treasure in the vessel of clay by making right choices.

remember

Do you not know that your body is a temple of the Holy Spirit, who is in you, whom you have received from God?

1 Corinthians 6:19
NIV

>> Look at your hands. Meditate on all the things hands can do, both good and bad. Dedicate the work of your hands to God.

#22

Practice the Inner Smile

> *I have stilled and quieted myself, just as a small child is quiet with its mother.*
>
> Psalm 131:2 NLT

smile

You may have heard that it takes more muscles to frown than to smile. Researchers now say that a smile can actually send signals to your body to produce chemicals that lift your mood. A smile can come from the inside, too. With the calmness and peace of a gentle smile, learn to detach from critical thoughts and bring the sunshine of acceptance into each situation.

When you are feeling stressed out, imagine that you are smiling at your current situation, bathing it in God's love. Smile within your own heart and then let the radiance of that inner smile be seen on your face.

>> When you are facing a stressful situation, use the concept of an inner smile to step back from the problem and bathe it in God's love.

#23

Get Your Beauty Sleep

A calm spirit in a rested body is a beautiful thing. Are you getting enough sleep, or do you try to cram too many things into each day? If you're tired, frazzled, and overcommitted, it's time to cut back on your busy schedule and make time for the things that count.

Hours of sleep before midnight are more rejuvenating, so an earlier bedtime can pay off in greater energy during the day. If you are not getting enough sleep, decide to modify your habits. Sleep is a gift from God. If you make restful sleep a priority, you'll reap energetic and spiritual benefits.

sleep

It is useless for you to work so hard from early morning until late at night, anxiously working for food to eat; for God gives rest to his loved ones.

Psalm 127:2 NLT

>> Go to bed an hour earlier tonight. Aim for six to eight hours of restful sleep each night.

#24

Take Regular Stress Breaks During the Day

> *If you know certain meetings or professional activities stress you out, plan a stress break... that will allow you to return to work more focused.*
>
> Robert Arnot

breaks

When your day feels hectic and out of control, it's vitally important to give yourself simple time-outs for stress relief. Escape from the office for a brief walk. Drink a glass of water or fruit juice. Renew your energy with exercise. Refresh your spirit with a brief time of prayer and meditation. Make room for God to speak timeless wisdom in the midst of your time crunch.

It's easy to get caught up in a fast-paced environment and forget to take care of your own needs. But including simple breaks in your day can refresh your body, renew your perspective, and replenish your spirit.

>> Remember to take frequent stress breaks during a busy day. Take a few minutes for prayer, for exercise, for hydration, and to regain perspective.

#25

Seek Spiritual Solutions to Your Problems

There is a spiritual root to every problem in your life. The outer situation points to an inner struggle within you. Even when a problem seems to be caused by a person or situation that is out of your control, your response is a spiritual response. Will you react with anger or understanding? Will you choose judgment or forgiveness?

If you want to find the spiritual solution to your problem, take it before God in prayer. Make a commitment to listen, and then to act on the wisdom you receive. Approaching a problem in the spirit of prayer will reveal spiritual insight.

seek

If you know the right thing to do and don't do it, that, for you, is evil.

James 4:17
THE MESSAGE

>> Set aside a time to pray about a specific problem that has been bothering you. Look for the spiritual solution.

#26
Clear Clutter

*I'm running hard for
the finish line. I'm
giving it everything
I've got. No sloppy
living for me!*

1 Corinthians 9:26
THE MESSAGE

clear

Is your desk piled high with paperwork? Is your purse or briefcase disorganized? Does your closet look like a tornado hit it? Does clutter make your life feel like a constant obstacle course? Clutter and disorganization can distract you and waste your energy.

Make a decision to begin clearing clutter in your life. Clearing the clutter of old attitudes, grudges, and negativity will also cleanse your spirit. When you clean out a closet, attend to paperwork, and organize your personal life, you'll find that you have more energy to focus on the things that are important to you.

>> Organize one small area of clutter: a shelf, a desk drawer, an overflowing in-basket, the pile of stuff that needs to be recycled.

#27

Keep a Gratitude Journal

Practicing gratitude as a way of life can show you how great and rich are the blessings in your life. Simple things like birdsong in the morning, sunlight through a window, a phone call from a friend, a kiss on the cheek—all can color your day a brighter shade of love, if you are aware of them.

A daily gratitude journal can be a wonderful reminder of God's blessings in your life. Just before you go to bed at night, list five blessings you received during the day. Soon you'll have a history of many days filled with gifts from the hand of God.

journal

Reflect upon your present blessings, of which every man has many; not on your past misfortunes, of which all men have some.

Charles Dickens

>> Create a daily gratitude journal. Write down five things you are grateful for each day.

#28
Organize Your Day

> *Order means*
> *light and peace,*
> *inward liberty*
> *and free command*
> *over oneself;*
> *order is power.*
>
> Henri Frederic Amiel

organize

It sounds simple and obvious to say that organizing your day can make things less stressful. But how many times have you missed an appointment or been late for a deadline because you were disorganized and let the day get away from you?

Take the time first thing in the morning—or last thing the night before—to plan your day. Make a to-do list and prioritize your actions. Don't forget to include time on your priority list for prayer and relaxation. You'll discover that being organized liberates you, freeing you to focus on the things that are most important to you.

>> Buy a personal calendar or organizer and use it for appointments, record keeping, and daily goals.

#29

Transform Your Thinking

What does it mean to transform your thinking? One way is to become aware of your thoughts and to actively choose to think better thoughts. Get out of a negative mental rut and decide to think about higher things. Stop going over why things went wrong or how someone hurt you. Choose to move from negative thoughts into more positive and creative thoughts. Replace complaints with praise.

Ask God to help you transform your thinking. When you find yourself dwelling on what's wrong, ask him to help you find what's right in every situation. Allow the light of love to transform your thoughts.

transform

Do not be conformed to this world, but be transformed by the renewing of your mind, that you may prove what is that good and acceptable and perfect will of God.

Romans 12:2 NKJV

>> When you find yourself thinking negatively, create a positive affirmation to replace the negative talk.

#30

Create Joy and Anticipation

> *Everything is possible for him who believes.*
>
> Mark 9:23 NIV

joy

God gave you the gift of imagination. You use it every day, even if you don't consider yourself "imaginative." You can use your imagination negatively to conjure up worst-case scenarios. Scenes of disaster and sirens screaming in the night and thieves breaking in may play over and over in your head.

Or you can use your imagination to focus on the good and to create new possibilities. You can create joy and anticipation instead of dread and anxiety. Let the Creator guide your imagination so that you can focus your energy on imagining a best-case scenario for your life.

>> Watch your imagination today. Every time you imagine a negative scenario, replace that thought with a faith-filled, positive scenario.

#31

Invest in a Massage

Athletes, dancers, overstressed homemakers, and busy executives have discovered the benefits of therapeutic massage for relieving stress, soothing sore muscles, and enhancing mental and emotional well-being. Invest in your health, and you'll reap benefits in mental clarity and energy. You'll discover more energy for cultivating the spiritual side of life as well.

There are many kinds of therapeutic massage available at health spas, clinics, and athletic facilities. You can also do simple self-massage at home. Refresh your feet with peppermint foot lotion, or soothe aching shoulders with a gentle hand-massage.

massage

Dear friend, I am praying that all is well with you and that your body is as healthy as I know your soul is.

3 John 2 NLT

>> Invest in a chair massage or a full-body massage with a massage therapist.

relax

101 ways to relax

eat

imagine

laugh

support

and reduce stress

honor

nourish

listen

#32

Cultivate the Art of Contentment

> *Be content with who you are, and don't put on airs. God's strong hand is on you; he'll promote you at the right time. Live carefree before God; he is most careful with you.*
>
> 1 Peter 5:6–7
> THE MESSAGE

contentment

You live in a consumer society that feeds on fears of scarcity and feelings of desire. Ads are created to fuel your desires for more or to push your buttons of insecurity. "Buy this lipstick and you'll attract the man of your dreams!" "Drive this car and you will be strong and powerful!" The seductive images speak to your subconscious, telling you that more is never enough.

Cultivating contentment is an antidote to toxic desires. Choose to delight in the gifts God has already given you. Enjoy the simple things in life: sunsets, delicious food, loving friends and family, beautiful flowers, and peaceful pleasures.

>> Spend an evening at home enjoying a simple meal and quiet activities.

#33

Let Love Be Your Inspiration

God is Love. Love is the energy that created the universe. When you are looking for lasting motivation, love is what will keep you going through thick and thin. When you do something in the spirit of love, you come from the real essence of who you are and what God created you to be.

Love others. And love your work. Life is much less stressful when you love what you do. Even if you are not doing what you love, you can still choose to do it with love. With love as your inspiration, you'll discover that you can move mountains.

love

The whole point of what we're urging is simply love — love uncontaminated by self-interest and counterfeit faith, a life open to God.

1 Timothy 1:5
THE MESSAGE

>> Meditate on the famous "love chapter" of the Bible: 1 Corinthians 13. How can you apply its wisdom to your daily life?

#34

Get Out in the Fresh Air

Climb the mountains and get good tidings. The winds will blow their own freshness into you, and the storms their energy, while cares will drop away from you like the leaves of Autumn.

John Muir

out

If you've been closeted indoors too long, your thoughts get as stuffy as the closed rooms you've been living in. It's time to get out and let the wind blow through your hair, the sun shine on your face, and the fresh air give vigor to your attitude.

Step outside and let the outdoors remind you that life is larger and airier and freer than the enclosed world you've been immured in. Watch a squirrel scrambling through leaves, intent on its business. Remember that life is rich and full and mysterious. God provided nature to share secrets of renewal with those who will take time to listen.

>> Walk outdoors today. Pick up five pretty leaves or rocks. Take them home to remind yourself of God's bounty and your creative potential.

#35

Take One Positive Action

Sometimes a desired goal may feel like an overwhelming process, far beyond your strength and ability. But a wall is built brick by brick, and a goal is reached step by step. You may think you have to make spectacular leaps, but baby steps are the surest way to reach your goal. Just as a bricklayer patiently adds one brick at a time to the wall he is building, so one positive action after another will help you create your dream.

It takes faith and courage. Yet each simple step leads to the next step. If you keep walking, you'll eventually reach your goal.

action

Even if you had faith as small as a mustard seed you could say to this mountain, "Move from here to there," and it would move. Nothing would be impossible.

Matthew 17:20–21
NLT

>> Write out the steps you think you need to take to reach a cherished goal. Pick one and do it.

#36

Lighten Up

For health and the constant enjoyment of life, give me a keen and ever present sense of humor; it is the next best thing to an abiding faith in providence.

George B. Cheever

lighten

Do you sometimes believe that being an adult means taking yourself too seriously? It's easy to get caught up in the "busy and important" syndrome of having no time for fun, no energy for humor. But Jesus taught that children are closer than self-important adults to understanding the kingdom of God.

When your interior weather is heavy, dark, and gloomy, bring a little lightness into your life. Let the sunshine of a smile, the lightness of laughter, and the joy of a childlike attitude bring brightness to your life. Play with children and learn from them. Lighten up and let the sunshine in.

>> Buy a coloring book and some crayons. Let yourself be a child again and enjoy creating something simple.

#37

Watch Your Self Talk

What gets more results—praise or criticism? People respond to praise, while constant criticism eventually discourages them from even trying. Now think about how you talk to yourself. Is your inner commentary an unending litany of criticism and put-downs? Do you say cruel things to yourself that you would never say to anyone else?

You are acceptable in the eyes of God. If God can see you with so much love, then you can learn to treat yourself with more honor. Give yourself credit for trying. Be kind and gentle with yourself. You'll find that life is easier with thoughts of encouragement and love.

watch

> *Growth begins when we start to accept our own weakness.*
>
> Jean Vanier

>> Pay attention to your inner dialogue. Do you judge yourself harshly when you make mistakes? Choose loving and encouraging thoughts instead.

#38

Take Time to Savor Your Accomplishment

> *Well-spoken words bring satisfaction; well-done work has its own reward.*
>
> Proverbs 12:14
> THE MESSAGE

savor

You did it! You accomplished your goal and did what you said you would do. But before you rush off to do the next thing on your list of things to do, take time to celebrate this accomplishment. Savor this moment. Give yourself credit for a job well done.

Sounds simple, doesn't it? But how often have you focused on everything you have yet to accomplish instead of seeing how much you have already done? Give yourself a chance to pause and acknowledge an accomplishment. Celebration makes it sweeter and more meaningful. You can then continue on, refreshed and renewed.

>> Hold a mini-celebration for an accomplished goal. Call a friend and say, "I did it!" Share your victory before you move on.

#39

Be On Time

Rushing out the door, you realize you're going to be late again. Is this is a common scenario in your life? Chronic lateness is a symptom of being out of sync, and it catches you up in a whirlwind of tardiness. Ask God to help you reset your inner clock and enter divine timing. Allow the Spirit to help you find a balance between trying to do too much and letting things slide, between being too early and being too late.

Being on time is a way to practice divine timing so you can be fully present wherever you are, centered in God's will for your life.

time

> *Better three hours too soon, than one minute too late.*
>
> William Shakespeare

>> Make it your intention to be five minutes early to your next appointment. Ask God to help you follow through on your intention.

#40
Let Go and Let God

> The One who called you is completely dependable. If he said it, he'll do it!
>
> 1 Thessalonians 5:24
> THE MESSAGE

let go

Sometimes life feels like a wrestling match. You've struggled and struggled to solve a problem or reach a cherished goal, yet never seem to overcome the situation or achieve your heart's desire. When you come to the limits of your strength and ability, call on God.

When you've done the best you can, let go and leave the results up to God. The secret of surrender frees you from a performance mentality. You are not responsible for running the world— God is. You do your part and trust that God will take it from there. You'll discover that God has a better idea.

>> Plant paper-white narcissus and watch the miracle of life unfold. Remember that you plant, but the creative energies of God make them grow.

#41
Prioritize

Everybody's schedule seems to be packed nowadays. And everyone seems to be overwhelmed with everything that has to be accomplished. You have so many worthwhile activities that it's hard to say no. You don't want to miss out on any good thing.

schedule

But if you are frazzled by trying to keep up with your own busy schedule, the things that are most important tend to get lost in the shuffle. Call a time-out and reexamine your priorities. Ask for God's guidance. Decide what is most important to you, and make that your highest priority. Sometimes you get more out of life by doing less.

I believe half the unhappiness in life comes from people being afraid to go straight at things.

William J. Locke

>> Write out your goals for this week and for the coming year. Make sure your week includes doing something toward achieving long-term goals.

#42

Seek Serenity

Speak, move, act in peace, as if you were in prayer. In truth, this is prayer.

François Fénelon

serenity

A still lake reflects the sky like a mirror. A calm spirit reflects the love of God. When your emotional seas are stormy, this is the time to ask Christ to calm the waters and speak peace to your soul. Seek serenity of spirit through time away in prayer, solitude, and intimate moments with God.

Moving your body in a regular rhythm through walking or other exercise can also help calm strong emotions, taking you out of the frustrating situation so you can regain perspective. You can also seek serenity by getting out into nature or spending time away from crowds in a quiet place.

>> Consider adding a fountain or an aquarium to your home; the sound of flowing water or the sight of swimming fish provides a serene background.

#43

Carry Inspiration with You

Inspiring words are reminders of what's important in life. An apt quotation or a verse of Scripture can lift your heart and help you stay the course. One way to carry inspiration wherever you go is to write a treasured quotation on a card and carry it with you.

Another way to carry inspiration with you is to memorize meaningful words. Choose a section of Scripture and learn it by heart. Psalm 23, the Beatitudes, and the Lord's Prayer have been perennial favorites, offering comfort and encouragement in the midst of life's challenges. Words known by heart will be remembered in times of need.

inspiration

I have hidden your word in my heart that I might not sin against you.

Psalm 119:11 NIV

>> Write a favorite quotation or Bible verse on a card and place it in your wallet or purse for instant inspiration.

#44

Listen to the Wisdom of Silence

Outward silence is indispensable for the cultivation and improvement of inner silence.

Madame Guyon

silence

This is a noisy society, filled with the sound of machines, the buzz of conversation, and the music and talk of television and radio. You need time to be away from all the noise. A quiet hour spent with God will replenish your spirit and give you access to your own inner wisdom.

Set aside a quiet time in the morning to be silent in God's presence. Let go of all the chatter and opinions and to-do lists; just be with God in the silence. Allow the silence to fill your inner emptiness. Consider spending an afternoon in silence to nurture your soul.

>> Create a personal mini-retreat for an afternoon or morning of silence, prayer, and meditation.

#45

Serve Others Through Simple Acts of Kindness

It doesn't have to be a flamboyant act of self-sacrifice. A little thoughtful act will do. Simple acts of kindness grease the wheels of life and make the world a more pleasant place to live. Holding a door open for someone, letting another in line before you at the grocery checkout, buying flowers to share with a friend, offering an encouraging word, or sending a letter or a card—any of these small acts of kindness can make someone's day more pleasant.

Jesus was not above being a servant. Be like him and honor others with simple kindness today. It will warm your heart, too.

serve

> *Whoever gives one of these little ones only a cup of cold water in the name of a disciple, assuredly, I say to you, he shall by no means lose his reward.*
>
> Matthew 10:42
> NKJV

>> Do one act of kindness today. Send a card, make a phone call, speak an encouraging word, give an anonymous gift of money.

#46

Overcome Fear with Love

There is no fear in love. But perfect love drives out fear, because fear has to do with punishment. The one who fears is not made perfect in love.

1 John 4:18 NIV

love

Fear is like a hand clutching your throat. You're afraid to breathe, afraid to move, paralyzed by images of scarcity, loneliness, failure, and lack. Fear blinds you to your own inner resources. Fear shouts so loud that you cannot hear God's whispered promises of love.

You can overcome fear by choosing love. Love is more powerful than fear. Love is the light that drives away the shadows of fear. Affirm that the love of God sustains you. Make choices based on love instead of fear. When you choose to respond to life with actions driven by love, fear no longer has power over you.

>> When you're afraid of scarcity, tithe your money. When you're afraid of loneliness, reach out to others.

#47

Choose Life

Sometimes playing it safe is a form of death. You become ossified when you are too set in your ways. You were created to grow. You need the challenge of something new in your daily activities and in your walk with God.

To be fully alive means that you don't have all the answers because life is larger and more wonderful than you can yet imagine. When you say yes to life, you are saying yes to the unknowns. The unknowns are where the growing edge is, where life and creativity are most fertile and abundant. Choose life, and life will choose you, too.

life

Be not afraid of life. Believe that life is worth living, and your belief will help create the fact.

William James

>> Challenge yourself by learning or doing something new: Meet new people, learn a new skill, take a trip to a new place.

reach

101 ways to relax

remember

let go

lighten up

watch

and reduce stress

act

renew

reexamine

#48

Accept What Is

Wait on the LORD;
be of good courage,
and He shall
strengthen your
heart; wait, I say,
on the LORD!

Psalm 27:14 NKJV

accept

You can waste a lot of energy fighting the facts. You may be sick or have financial limitations. You might have had a misunderstanding with a friend or loved one. You've noticed more gray hairs on your head. Your job might not be as fulfilling as it once was.

Accepting that these conditions exist is not admitting defeat. It is acknowledging what you have to work with. Surrender your disappointment to God. Allow room for creative responses to arise instead of holding on tightly to either-or scenarios. When you have faced and accepted what is, you can make wiser choices in each situation.

>> As an act of faith and trust, thank God for the thing that is troubling you and ask for wisdom in dealing with it.

#49

Fast for Renewal and Energy

You fill your stomach with too much food and feel bloated and lethargic. You fill your schedule with too many activities and feel scattered and exhausted. It's time for a fast.

Fasting does not mean that you have to be an ascetic who withdraws from the world or stops eating. Cutting back and simplifying can be a simple form of fasting. Exchange heavy foods for lighter vegetables and fruits for a day or two. Cut back on your commitments to give yourself some needed time off. Food tastes better when your palate is clear. Life is more enjoyable when you've had time away with God.

renewal

Abstinence is the mother of health. A few ounces of privation is an excellent recipe for any ailment.

Anthony Grassi

>> Do a juice and vegetable fast for a day to cleanse your system. Retreat for a day to rest your spirit.

#50

Light a Candle

I live and love in God's peculiar light.

Michelangelo

light

It's a simple little ritual, but it can be meaningful. Lighting a candle can help you set aside sacred time in your day. Jews mark the beginning of Sabbath by lighting candles and saying a prayer. You can mark a Sabbath moment by lighting a candle and taking time out for prayer and meditation.

The candle is a reminder that this time is different from the rest of your day. It is a time set apart for you to converse with God and bring your cares before him. As long as the candle burns, you are in a sacred space and a sacred time.

>> Buy a special candle to light for your times of meditation.

#51

Worship with Others

It is wonderful to worship God when you are home alone. Even more wonderful is gathering together with other people for communal worship. The music, the singing, and the gathering together create an energy that uplifts and inspires. You are no longer a spiritual Lone Ranger, but instead a fellow traveler with many other pilgrims.

A worship service or a fellowship meeting to serve the community of faith is a rich counterpoint to your personal spiritual time. You will find encouragement, understanding, and joy when you spend time with others in worship, service, and praise.

worship

Come, let us bow down in worship, let us kneel before the LORD our Maker.

Psalm 95:6 NIV

>> Attend a worship service this week.

#52

Listen to Soothing Music

> *Music strikes in me a profound contemplation of the First Composer.*
>
> Thomas Browne

listen

Music can have a profound effect on energy levels and mood. It may even strengthen your immune system. Music can energize with an upbeat rhythm or soothe with mellow sounds. Robert McDonald, an expert on neurolinguistic programming, said, "All music is inherently intended to be therapeutic. Real therapy, which is spiritual, and music like Gregorian chant are aligned."

Create your own music therapy session by choosing soothing and uplifting music. Let the sound and the spirit of the music heal, comfort, and inspire you.

>> Take a time-out to listen to music that moves you. Put the headphones on, close your eyes, and let God use the music to speak to your spirit.

#53

Come from Your Highest Self

The Bible speaks of a higher self and a lower self. Galatians 6:22–23 outlines the fruits of the Spirit, the outward signs of an inward grace. Love, joy, peace, patience, kindness, goodness, faithfulness, gentleness, and self-control grow in your life when you choose to approach life from your higher self instead of from your lower nature.

The higher self sees the bigger picture and is patient. The higher self is compassionate and gentle with others. Love and forgiveness replace fear and judgment. The inner Christ-nature connects you to God, bringing clarity and peace to your heart.

come

The human soul is God's treasury, out of which he coins unspeakable riches. Thoughts and feelings, desires and yearnings, faith and hope — these are the most precious things which God finds in us.

Henry Ward
Beecher

>> Do a word study on each of the nine fruits of the Spirit listed in Galatians 6:22–23 and see what else the Bible has to say about these spiritual qualities.

#54

Forgive Others

Live creatively, friends. If someone falls into sin, forgivingly restore him, saving your critical comments for yourself. You might be needing forgiveness before the day's out.

Galatians 6:1
THE MESSAGE

forgive

How much energy do you waste on anger? What good does it do for you to hold a grudge against someone who hurt you? The answers to these questions may seem obvious, but emotions often cloud the issue, making forgiveness seem counterintuitive, and making holding a grudge the most natural thing in the world.

The Lord's Prayer reads, "Forgive us our debts, as we forgive our debtors" (Matthew 6:12 NKJV). Today, make a commitment to choose forgiveness. It may take time to work out what forgiveness means in each situation, but the intention to forgive is the first step toward freedom and peace.

>> Write the name of someone you need to forgive. Now tear up or burn that piece of paper as a symbol of releasing your pain to God in forgiveness.

#55

Forgive Yourself

"Ow! That was stupid." "Why did I do that?" "What was I thinking when I made that mistake?" "I regret that with all my heart." Do these phrases sound familiar? If you find them going around in your head, it's time to drop the baggage, forgive yourself, and move on.

You have already been forgiven by God, long before you knew you needed forgiveness. Now it's time to take those promises of grace seriously and forgive yourself. You made the choices you made and you cannot unmake them. But you now can make better choices if you forgive yourself and trust in God's grace.

forgive

As far as sunrise is from sunset, [God] has separated us from our sins.
Psalm 103:12
THE MESSAGE

>> Commit to a fresh start. Instead of criticizing yourself, encourage your heart with praise and gratitude for God's immeasurable forgiving grace.

#56

Take Yourself Out

Play is the business of childhood, and its continuation in later years is the prolongation of youth.
Walter Rauschenbusch

o u t

You put in a full week of work. You run errands, accomplish as much as you possibly can, and check off most of your to-do list (there's always more to do, so give yourself credit for what you've already done). Take time for some rest and relaxation.

Don't let self-nurture always be last on your list of things to do. All work and no play is a surefire recipe for burnout. Make a date and take yourself out for a good time. Even the trash gets taken out once a week. Take time away to recharge your batteries. Do something you love, just for fun.

>> Set aside a time on your calendar for play. Solo or with someone else, make sure you keep your date with yourself.

#57

Drop Perfectionism

It's one thing to love excellence; it's another thing to drive yourself crazy attempting to be perfect. You may tell yourself that no one is perfect, but do you really believe that? Or do you keep picking at yourself for not meeting your own exacting standards? If you're too hard on yourself, more than likely you'll be hard on others as well.

drop

Perfectionism is another way of trying to control life. But life is much larger than your limited ideas of what it should be. Drop your unmet expectations and open yourself to the serendipities of life. Allow the perfection of grace to surprise you.

> *Striving for excellence motivates you; striving for perfection is demoralizing.*
>
> Harriet Braiker

>> Celebrate the grace of imperfection: a clumsy puppy, weather-beaten wood, antiques worn by time, a two-year-old with an ice-cream cone.

#58

Immerse Yourself in Something You Love

> The beauty of all things is derived from the divine beauty.
>
> Saint Thomas Aquinas

immerse

Sometimes the to-do list is too full of "should" and not enough of "I'd love to!" It's a fine thing to take care of business and meet your obligations. But you also need something for the heart.

Do you love the feel of a good horse under you? Do you dream of picking fragrant roses in your own garden? Would you love to explore a different side of town? Are you thrilled with putting paint on canvas or words on paper? Music, architecture, skiing, the stock market, livestock—what do you love? These all are creative gifts from God. Are you willing to enjoy them?

>> List ten things you would love to do "if you only had the time."
Do one of them.

#59

Honor What Is Most Important to You

Some people have trouble saying no. They'll say yes to everything and everybody until they can't call their lives their own. But they can't say no because they're afraid it's too "selfish" or too "mean." After all, doesn't serving God mean serving everybody else, too?

No is an important word for your vocabulary. *No* can help you sort priorities so that your time and energy are used for the highest purposes instead of being drained away by unthinking need. Honor what is important to you by being willing to say no to requests that do not honor your highest purpose.

honor

There is really only one thing worth being concerned about. Mary has discovered it — and I won't take it away from her.

Luke 10:42 NLT

>> Read the story of Mary and Martha in Luke 10:38–42. Think about how you balance accommodating others and serving your highest purpose in life.

#60

Tap the Wisdom of the Body

The body is matter, but it is God's creation. When it is neglected or scoffed at, God himself is insulted.

Michel Quoist

wisdom

Your body is wiser than you realize. It is God's gift to you. Your body knows what you need. It's attuned to your surroundings, too.

Pay attention to physical signals. Your body tells you to rest when you're upset, knowing that sleep will give you a new perspective. If you push yourself too hard, illness makes you stop and reexamine your course of action. Your gut feelings don't lie—researchers have even discovered that there are brain cells in your intestine! Your body is fearfully and wonderfully made, a marvelous intuitive instrument that can instruct you with earthly wisdom, if you will listen.

>> The next time you have a "gut feeling" about a situation, pay attention to what your body is telling you instead of dismissing it with "logic."

#61

Find a Prayer Partner

When you are facing difficult times or struggling with problems, prayer can help you find your way. Sharing with a prayer partner and praying for one another can be even more encouraging.

Ask God to lead you to the right person to pray with. You want someone who will be supportive and an equal in prayer, not someone who will drain you or make you feel like a spiritual inferior. If you can enlist a dear friend who shares many of the same struggles and temptations, all the better. Plan to get together on a regular basis and pray for each other daily.

partner

Comfort each other and edify one another, just as you also are doing.

1 Thessalonians 5:11
NKJV

>> Commit to meeting with a friend for prayer. Check in with each other on at least a weekly basis.

#62

Bask in the Sun

Light is sweet; it's wonderful to see the sun!

Ecclesiastes 11:7 NLT

bask

Though overexposure to sunlight can be unhealthy, it's now been discovered (or rediscovered) that a moderate amount of direct sunlight is beneficial. The body needs sunlight to manufacture vitamin D. Light not only lifts your mood, but it is also a depression preventive.

Cats love to bask in the sun, absorbing the warmth of the sun's rays. Take some time and emulate those wise animals. As you close your eyes and turn your face to the sunlight, imagine that the warmth is not only from the sun, but also from the light and love and warmth of God. Pause and praise as you bask in the sun.

>> Spend a half-hour basking in the sun, just sitting and thinking and being.

#63

Give Something Away

Scarcity thinking will make you want to clutch tight to everything you own. The flow of abundance runs on a different energy—that of generosity and a sense of plenitude. Giving something away renews this spirit of abundance within you.

Everything you have is a gift from God. Everything you give away is a gift to God. Are you a cheerful and generous giver? You can start small and simply. Clean out a closet. Give a plant from your garden. Give your time to a favorite charity. Best of all, give the gift of your best self to everyone you meet.

give

Whoever has this world's goods, and sees his brother in need, and shuts up his heart from him, how does the love of God abide in him?

1 John 3:17 NKJV

>> Clean out your closet and give clothes you no longer use to a favorite charity.

accept

101 ways to relax

surrender

cut back

worship

forgive

and reduce stress

commit

recharge

play

#64
Sleep On It

> *Jesus knows we must come apart and rest awhile, or else we may just plain come apart.*
>
> Vance Havner

sleep

Your body is telling you what your mind refuses to acknowledge. You want to wrestle with this problem all night until you find an answer. So you pump yourself up with caffeine and keep going around and around in circles over the same old territory.

Listen to your body. It's time to take a break and get some rest. The problem will still be there in the morning. There's nothing more you can do about it tonight. Sleep on it. You'll have a better perspective when you've had some rest. Let the angels sing to you in your dreams and whisper wisdom for tomorrow's decisions.

>> The next time you're wrestling with a problem or a big decision, sleep on it. You'll have a clearer perspective when you're rested.

#65

Give Yourself a Bouquet

There are all kinds of sensible choices you can make to take care of yourself. But there is something so delightfully enchanting about treating yourself to fresh flowers. They are not useful in a utilitarian sense, but they feed the soul's desire for beauty and bounty.

The unfolding of a rose is a miracle, reminding you of how you are unfolding like a rose under the sun of God's love. Lilies are fragrant, reminding you that life is sweet. A big bouquet, a single rose, or wildflowers gathered from the side of the road— say it with flowers and take joy in creation's sweet pleasures.

bouquet

> *Remember that the most beautiful things in the world are the most useless: peacocks and lilies, for instance.*
>
> John Ruskin

>> Stop at a flower stand and pick your favorite bouquet. Buy it, take it home, and enjoy it.

#66

Get Your Hands Dirty

The LORD God had planted a garden in the east, in Eden; and there he put the man he had formed.

Genesis 2:8 NIV

garden

There is something so satisfying about putting your hands in good brown earth. Creating and caring for a garden is good for the soul. You can create your own personal Eden, whether you have a few acres or just a few flowerpots.

It is exciting to plant a seed, water it, and watch it grow into a beautiful plant. As you cultivate your garden it will teach you lessons about the nature of life and spirit and growth. Gardeners connect to God through soil and seed, cultivation and harvest. You'll learn patience and reap satisfaction when you get your hands dirty in a garden.

>> Take a trip to the garden-supply store and start planning your garden.

#67

Discover the Sacred in the Ordinary

"Just an ordinary day," you sigh. Nothing special, merely commonplace. Take another look. Yes, it's the same sun that shines every day, but it is bright with God's love and care. That coffee or tea you're drinking took many hands and much human ingenuity to land in your morning cup.

Go outside and enjoy the weather. Rain or shine, the blessings fall on everyone—the good and the bad alike. Spirituality is not something for Sundays only, and you don't need to lock God in a cathedral. This beautiful, heartbreaking, wonderful world is an ongoing love letter from God. Read it!

discover

Earth's crammed with heaven, and every common bush afire with God.

Elizabeth Barrett Browning

>> Look for the little miracles of life that are all around you: seeds sprouting, flowers blooming, faces smiling.

#68

Be Kind and Compassionate

If you judge people, you do not have time to love them.

Mother Teresa

kind

Are you too critical? Do you tend to judge yourself and others, focusing on flaws and behavior you disapprove of? Although a passion for excellence is good, most critical thoughts have little to do with improvement, and more to do with self—self-justification and condemnation of self or others.

Take it easy on yourself. Be compassionate to others. Remember that you are doing the best you can with what you understand at the time. Give yourself room to grow. Believe that God is helping others grow too. Give the gift of compassionate grace and leave judgment to God.

>> The next time you find yourself being critical of a situation, another person, or yourself, stop and choose compassion instead.

#69

Pray for Someone Who Is Struggling

When you get caught up in your own problems, one of the best ways to find a larger perspective is to focus on the struggles and needs of others. Prayer takes you into the presence of God, reminding you of his ability to transform even the most difficult problem into a blessing.

When you pray for a friend with cancer, your common cold seems more bearable. Praying for people in a war-torn country helps you see your own neighborhood in new light. Prayer changes you as well as the situation, and praying for someone else releases God's grace in ways you cannot imagine.

pray

When we are weighed down with troubles, it is for your benefit and salvation! For when God comforts us, it is so that we, in turn, can be an encouragement to you.

2 Corinthians 1:6
NLT

>> Send a card or letter to let someone know you are remembering them in your prayers.

#70

Be Open to God's Surprises

> *Great opportunities come to all, but many do not know they have met them. The only preparation to take advantage of them is simple fidelity to watch what each day brings.*
>
> Albert E. Dunning

surprises

Do you get frustrated at interruptions in your day? Everyone does. Even pleasant surprises, like a phone call from a friend, may feel like an interruption when you are busy and have other plans. But what if you looked at interruptions as signs of grace and whispers from God?

You can view life's surprises and detours as divine gifts. You may have planned a productive morning when an unexpected emergency calls you away. But taking care of that emergency may be the most important work you accomplish. Something unexpected may turn out to be a divine appointment. Be open and let God surprise you.

>> Surprise someone with a thoughtful action or a small gift: a bouquet, a card, a phone call, an offer to baby-sit, a casserole, a party.

#71

Retreat for Higher Perspective

Jesus and his disciples were familiar with high-pressure situations. During his ministry he was constantly calling the disciples away for retreat and renewal. Although the need was great and the crowds were demanding, it was vital that they get away to find a higher perspective.

No matter how busy you are or how many obligations you have to fulfill, you also need to renew and replenish your spirit. Time away with God is a necessity. A retreat—individual or group with fellow spiritual seekers—offers an opportunity to view your life from a higher perspective.

retreat

> [Jesus] said to them, "Come aside by yourselves to a deserted place and rest a while." For there were many coming and going, and they did not even have time to eat.
>
> Mark 6:31 NKJV

>> Consider going away for a day, a weekend, or even a week for a retreat by yourself or with others.

#72

Stop Comparing

We love in others what we lack in ourselves, and would be everything but what we are.

R. H. Stoddard

stop

You live in a society that loves to compare and judge. There are lists for the best dressed and the worst dressed. Schools grade on the curve. Contests and top-ten lists offer dozens of ways to rank people as successes or failures. You are encouraged to focus on performance and outer achievement.

God looks on the heart, not the outward appearance—and you can too. When you are tempted to start comparing yourself with others, shift your focus. Cherish your uniqueness and count your blessings. Love yourself and others by choosing compassion over comparison, love over judgment.

>> Do a kindness for someone you envy.

#73

Have a Good Cry

"Big boys don't cry." "Get over it." "Keep a stiff upper lip." "That's nothing to cry about." You've been told again and again that crying is immature, uncool, and a sign of unwanted weakness. You've been told wrong.

Tears are a wonderful emotional release. Tears of sorrow cleanse physical as well as emotional toxins from your system. Tears of joy allow emotion to heal body and soul. Let the tears flow. Allow yourself to feel and release your emotions instead of stuffing or denying them. Tears are a natural, God-given gift, created to help you process your emotions.

cry

> *The Sovereign LORD will wipe away the tears from all faces; he will remove the disgrace of his people from all the earth.*
>
> Isaiah 25:8 NIV

>> Don't be ashamed of your tears. If someone has hurt you, have a good cry. If you are moved, let the tears flow.

#74

Finding Rest in a Weary World

> Sabbath is a way of being in time where we remember who we are, remember what we know, and taste the gifts of spirit and eternity.
>
> Wayne Muller

rest

On the seventh day, God rested. Genesis is a reminder of the ancient rhythms of work and rest, creation and renewal. But modern humanity presses on to a different rhythm. The machine age encouraged people to work over-time. Now the computer age demands that you be available around the clock. There is constant pressure to keep going without stopping. You need to rediscover a Sabbath rest.

Sabbath is a time to rest and be with God, to enjoy the delights of being human. Rest, play, and enjoy being instead of doing. Rest from your labors and find renewal for your spirit.

>> Remember that you are a human being, not a human doing. Set aside regular time each week for rest, recreation, and prayer.

#75

Read a Good Book

Books offer a treasure chest of knowledge. A good book can expand your horizons, allow you to learn from another's experience, and help you grow spiritually. Reading is an investment in your education. A good book (or even a not-so-great book) can take you out of your everyday world, giving you a taste of other lives, other times, other places, other viewpoints and experiences.

Whether you read a devotional for a few minutes before bed or set aside an afternoon to lie on the couch and sink into a novel, reading a good book is a delightful way to widen your perspective on life.

r e a d

> *One can have knowledge without having wisdom, but one cannot have wisdom without having knowledge.*
>
> R. C. Sproul

>> Go to your local library or bookstore. Browse and find a book that moves, inspires, or delights you. Take it home and enjoy it.

#76

Focus on One Task Instead of Many

All good is gained by those whose thought and life are kept pointed to one main thing, not scattered abroad on a thousand.

Stephen McKenna

focus

Do you habitually try to do many things at once? It's called multitasking, but it can drive you crazy. When you are distracted by too many things to do, you dilute your energy. Think about what you can do to clear clutter and how you want to sort your priorities. Choose what's most important to you. Concentrate on one task and stay focused until it is completed. Then go on to the next task.

By focusing on one task or goal at a time, you harness the full energy of your mind. Being focused helps you accomplish more in the long run.

>> Clean up your work area. Prioritize your goals. Now concentrate on one task and put your whole heart into it.

#77

Listen to the Voice of Your Heart

The heart's wisdom transcends the mind's understanding. When you depend too heavily on "logic" you become out of balance. The heart is more than an emotional center; it is the center of gravity that balances you between heaven and earth. The heart has its own wisdom, and God's Spirit speaks most directly through the heart.

Listen to the voice of your heart, the inner light that is compassionate and loving. Obey those heartfelt impulses to give to another, spend more time with God, cultivate beauty, and nurture innocence. Let your heart lead more often than your head. Choose to be loving, and you will be loved.

listen

> *Keep vigilant watch over your heart; that's where life starts.*
>
> Proverbs 4:23
> THE MESSAGE

>> Write a letter to a friend or family member telling why you love and value him or her. Be specific.

#78

Commit to a Daily Quiet Time

If I have accomplished anything in the world, I attribute it to the fact that the first hour of every day of my life for years has been given to communion with God in secret prayer and the study of his word.

Earl Cairns

commit

If you want to develop a friendship, you need to spend time with your friend. If you want to develop your friendship with God, set aside a regular time for prayer, meditation, and spiritual reading. Spending quiet time alone with God every day can transform your life. Soon you will wonder how you got along without that intimate time dedicated to spiritual growth.

Many people find that starting their day with a devotional reading and time of prayer sets the tone for the rest of the day. Others find that evening prayer provides a benediction as they give thanks for the blessings of the day.

>> Buy a daily devotional book or Bible to give a simple structure to your quiet times with God.

#79

Celebrate the Little Things

The big things in life are important. Births, graduations, weddings, promotions, deaths, and life-changing events mark the changing seasons of life. But it's the little things that keep you going on ordinary days. Scrambled eggs and coffee, a smile from a stranger, a job well done, a hard day survived with grace—small miracles that are easily taken for granted make up the stuff of everyday life.

Celebrate the small things in life. Celebrate what you accomplished today. Celebrate the first daffodil in spring, the last rose of summer, and the fact that you are alive and breathing and blessed by God.

celebrate

Let them sacrifice thank offerings and tell of his works with songs of joy.

Psalm 107:22 NIV

>> Write your own personal prayer of gratitude and say it aloud to God.

sleep

101 ways to relax

give

plant

discover

pray

and reduce stress

be open

retreat

cry

#80

Practice Positive Faith: Expect the Best

> *A cheerful disposition is good for your health; gloom and doom leave you bone-tired.*
>
> Proverbs 17:22
> THE MESSAGE

expect

Henry Ford said it well: "Think you can, think you can't; either way, you'll be right." It's your willingness to practice a positive faith that overcomes your fears and doubts. Optimism strengthens faith. Negativity saps energy and often creates the very thing you dread.

A positive faith can move mountains. Romans 8:31 (NIV) reads, "If God is for us, who can be against us?" When you feel discouraged, say to yourself: "If God is for me, who can be against me?" Believe that the best is possible and see what God does through you.

>> Write an encouraging quotation or a promise from the Bible on an index card. Post it in a prominent place as a faith reminder.

#81

Know When Enough Is Enough

"Buy this!" "You won't be complete unless you own this!" "You need this!" The seductive voices of the consumer society urge you to overspend. But what use is a houseful of things you don't enjoy and never use? Did you really need another pair of shoes or the latest electronic gadget?

Learn to know when enough is enough. Instead of buying more things or stuffing your personal schedule with too many activities, simplify your life. Enjoy what you already own. Pare down your schedule so you can spend more time with loved ones and with God. A little moderation can bring great contentment.

enough

Godliness with contentment is great gain.

1 Timothy 6:6 NIV

>> Choose to declare a moratorium on buying things for a week. See how simple you can make your life.

#82

Sit and Stare

> *What we nurture in ourselves will grow. This is nature's eternal law.*
>
> Johann Wolfgang von Goethe

stare

You are busy and have a great deal to accomplish. The chores are always there, the to-do list never seems to grow shorter, and the demands on your time don't let up. After a while, your mind gets tired and your soul grows weary.

Try this simple remedy: Take a break, sit, stare, do nothing. Watch a thunderstorm roll through or a butterfly suck nectar from a flower. Look out the window at passing clouds or across the green grass to the horizon beyond. Be like a child—empty, open, and receptive to God's Spirit. Discover the secret of doing nothing in particular.

>> Take a few minutes to listen to the birds, watch the clouds move across the sky, and allow your heart and mind to rest in God.

#83

Try Some Hug Therapy

Studies show that babies who are touched and loved and held thrive, while babies who are not hugged or held enough do not grow as quickly. Adults need loving touch just as much as babies do. Hug therapy is an antidote to stress and loneliness.

Start with your family and close friends. Make sure that they get a fair share of your hugs. Children are wonderful huggers. From a fellowship meeting to a prayer circle, church is a great place for hugging. Volunteer to help sick children and newborns in hospitals that could use your gift of loving and gentle hug therapy.

hug

Loving God includes loving people. You've got to love both.

1 John 4:21
THE MESSAGE

>> Try to give at least one hug a day. Cuddle a child, hug a loved one, share hugs with friends.

#84
Trust the Process

Trust GOD from the bottom of your heart; don't try to figure out everything on your own. Listen for GOD's voice in everything you do, everywhere you go.
Proverbs 3:5–6
THE MESSAGE

trust

In a society focused on results and end products, it is easy to forget that you can't create without going through a process of creation. You may say you have a certain goal or end result in mind, but often the actual work may take you in another direction. And many times a seemingly messy detour becomes the path to something unexpected and wonderful.

Whether you are creating a work of art or a life, trust the process. Let go of your expectations and let what you are doing lead you from one step to another. Do your best and leave the results to God.

>> Do a creative project, such as building model airplanes or knitting, and watch the process unfold. Meditate on the processes unfolding in your life.

#85

Learn a Lesson from Dogs

You're strolling in the park, and here comes Fido, straining at the leash, sniffing and snuffling and oh, so happy to be out in the fresh air. Dog enthusiasm is unlimited. A dog loves life wholeheartedly, adoringly, without reservation or judgment, greeting each new scent or sight with boundless joy and radiant, unselfconscious glee. Everything encountered is a delightful gift from the hand of God.

Take note of this exuberant enthusiasm and apply it to your own view of life. Be open to the gifts of God, the small joys of living. Appreciate what is, and always be ready to receive whatever bounty the moment brings.

learn

> *Enthusiasm is the greatest asset in the world. It beats money and power and influence. It is no more or less than faith in action.*
>
> Henry Chester

>> Just for today, set aside your critical thoughts and see everything—good, bad, or indifferent—as a gift from the hand of God.

#86

Energize Yourself Through Regular Exerci

> *Exercise is the magic bullet for creating mental energy. Regular exercise elevates your overall month-to-month mood and feeling of optimism.*
>
> **Robert Arnot**

exercise

Researchers have found that exercise can shift a negative mood to a positive mood. Exercise energizes you and decreases the stress and tension that rob you of mental energy. For a short-term energy boost, a high-intensity work-out of twenty minutes or more will brighten your mental outlook, calm you down, and give you stamina for several hours. Long-term regular daily activity can help you overcome the effects of stress.

Steady, rhythmic exercise like walking and biking can give you immediate energy. Aerobics, strength training, meditative movement—try them all and see what you enjoy the most.

>> If you don't have a regular exercise routine, start one now. If you have one, try new ways of exercising to revitalize your routine.

#87

Create Pleasant Surroundings

It may sound obvious that pleasing sights, sounds, and aromas help reduce tension and help you feel better. But how many times have you settled for clutter and noise when, with minimal effort, you could have had beauty and order instead?

A loud television or a pounding stereo can frazzle your nerves with endless noise. Ugly, dirty, or cluttered surroundings make you feel scattered and distracted. Your soul responds to beauty. Your spirit needs quiet. The scent of fresh-baked bread, a beautifully set table, the loveliness of fresh flowers—these are soothing blessings that say you care about yourself.

create

> *There are certain things we feel to be beautiful and good, and we must hunger after them.*
>
> George Eliot

>> Open a window and get some fresh air. Put some calming music on the stereo. Set a bouquet of fresh flowers on a table.

#88

Cultivate a Childlike Heart

> *Jesus intervened:*
> *"Let the children*
> *alone, don't prevent*
> *them from coming to*
> *me. God's kingdom is*
> *made up of people*
> *like these."*
>
> Matthew 19:14
> THE MESSAGE

heart

A child looks with wonder at the world. Watch parents with young children on a nature walk. Mom and Dad have the walk mapped out, the destination clearly in mind. But Junior is interested in every detail along the way—a worm working its way across an asphalt road or a stick that's just the right size for throwing. A child has the eyes to see heaven in a wildflower and the world in a grain of sand.

When you are feeling world-weary, cultivate a sense of wonder and trust. Cultivate a childlike spirit, open to every gift of God, no matter how simple or commonplace.

>> Watch children at play. Remember the enchantment you knew as a child and open your heart to that sense of wonder once again.

#89

Don't Worry, Be Happy

The phrase "Be not afraid" is found more then three hundred times in the New Testament. Jesus said, "Do not worry about tomorrow, for tomorrow will worry about its own things" (Matthew 6:3–4 NKJV). Worry steals your energy. When you focus on what could go wrong, you miss out on what's going right.

When you are tempted to worry, exchange those heavy thoughts for some lighthearted praise and gratitude. Focus your thoughts on the fact that in this moment—right here and now—you are all right. Let tomorrow take care of itself. Set your worries aside, and enjoy what you have today.

happy

> *Worry weighs us down; a cheerful word picks us up.*
>
> Proverbs 12:25
> THE MESSAGE

>> Meditate on Psalm 23. If the Lord is your shepherd, what does that mean in the details of your life today?

#90

Find Comfort in God

The fundamental fact of existence is that this trust in God, this faith, is the firm foundation under everything that makes life worth living. It's our handle on what we can't see.

Hebrews 11:1
THE MESSAGE

comfort

Sometimes life can feel over-whelming. When terrifying events happen and terror strikes, seek comfort in a higher power. When finances are at a low ebb, take your worries to God in prayer. God is Love, and love is stronger than death. Offer your sorrow to that which is greater than you and find the peace that passes understanding. Exchange fear for faith by concentrating on the greatness of God.

Remember that God's Spirit is with you always, no matter what happens. You may not know why the hard times happen, but you do know whom you can trust in the midst of them.

>> Memorize a comforting Bible verse (such as Isaiah 43:2) for comfort when you are afraid.

#91

Play with Your Whole Heart

In a never-ending quest for a secure paycheck and steady job, it's easy to lose sight of what life is all about. Life should be a wonderful adventure, with high accomplishment and a spice of fun to give flavor to the whole dish. You know how to work hard. But do you know how to play well?

Play should be rejuvenating, allowing you to reach for fresh new ideas. Choose leisure-time activities that give you a sense of thrill and adventure. Take up new challenges that give you a natural high. Do something with your whole heart and let the fun be its own reward.

play

Let the righteous be glad; let them rejoice before God; yes, let them rejoice exceedingly.

Psalm 68:3 NKJV

>> Take up an active and challenging sport or hobby, one that rewards you with renewed confidence and joy.

#92

Avoid Procrastination

> *Procrastination is the thief of time.*
>
> Edward Young

avoid

Procrastination, putting off until tomorrow what should be done today, steals precious energy. Procrastination produces guilt because you know you should do something but you don't. It creates stress because the more you avoid doing the thing you dread, the larger it looms in your mind and the less energy you have for the rest of your life.

Choose to value your time by doing what needs to be done right now. Now is the time to take care of those undone chores and long-delayed tasks. By tackling those tasks, you'll clear the way to be ready to take needed action.

>> Set a simple goal for today and achieve that goal. Reward yourself with a small pleasure when you achieve the goal.

#93

Make Time and Space for Creativity

God has given you unique creative gifts. Use the play of creativity to relax and take a break from endless to-do lists. Doing creative projects—putting paint on canvas, shaping clay, knitting and weaving, gardening, woodworking—renews your soul and gives you a welcome respite from the stress of the workaday world.

Honor that creative potential within you. Make space for creative projects and interests in your home. Take time to nurture your creativity. Buy books on developing creativity and invest in classes that take you on new creative adventures. Allow room for creativity and watch your horizons widen and expand.

t i m e

People do not quit playing because they grow old. They grow old because they quit playing.

Oliver Wendell
Holmes

>> Set aside a special corner or a room for creative projects. Mark out creative appointments on your calendar—and keep them!

#94

Get Out of Your Rut

> *I've come to change everything, turn everything rightside up.*
>
> Luke 12:50
> THE MESSAGE

rut

If life has lost its savor and everything feels like a dull routine, you could be stuck in a rut. It's easy to resist change and defend your right to think the same old thoughts, do the same old things, and stick with the known instead of the unknown. Ruts can be comfortable.

Challenge yourself. Try something new. Expand your boundaries. Choose to get out of your rut and grow as a person. Let the new things you learn bring you into the flow of life. You'll feel invigorated. You'll discover that as you open to change, your spiritual life will also grow and expand.

>> Take a new route to work. Go to a new restaurant and order a new dish. Invest in a workshop or class.

#95

Play to Your Strengths

Everybody has strong and weak points. One person is a quiet introvert, another a free-spirited extrovert. One person can accomplish many tasks quickly, while another takes more time to do the work necessary.

Your temperament and talents are unique. Relax, enjoy your uniqueness, and stop comparing yourself unfavorably to others. Instead of wasting energy by stressing out on what you can't do, focus on what you're naturally good at. When someone else seems to work faster, accept that you work at your own pace. By concentrating on your strengths, you'll get better at what you do and have more fun doing it.

strengths

If fear is cultivated it will become stronger, if faith is cultivated it will achieve mastery.

John Paul Jones

>> Take a temperament test, such as the Myers-Briggs Type Indicator, to help you understand your own strengths.

expect

101 ways to relax

know

sit

hug

trust

and reduce stress

learn

energize

cultivate

#96

Say Yes to What You Love

It is the greatest shot of adrenaline to be doing what you've wanted to do so badly. You almost feel like you could fly without the plane.

Charles Lindbergh

yes

He was the first to fly the Atlantic solo and nonstop. Charles Lindbergh dreamed of extending the boundaries of flight. When he landed his plane, the *Spirit of St. Louis*, outside Paris on May 21, 1927, he became an international hero. He flew not for adulation or reward, but because he loved flying.

When you do something for love, it can feel like flying. It's been shown that people immersed in something they love are more relaxed, more creative, and better able to cope with the demands of living. Make time in your schedule to do the things you love. You'll enjoy life more.

>> Is there something that makes you feel as if you could "fly without the plane"? When was the last time you did it?

#97

Indulge Yourself

Self-discipline is an admirable trait and should be cultivated. But sometimes a small treat can work wonders for encouraging self-discipline when all the good intentions in the world won't. The kid in you still loves chocolate ice-cream cones (or tutti-frutti or rocky road or any one of a zillion flavors).

Tiny treats and small indulgences make perfect rewards for goals achieved and jobs well done. Indulgences can be as simple as a piece of chocolate or a fragrant bubble bath. A simple pleasure can ease a stressful day. Give yourself a gold star for good behavior—and indulge in five minutes of pure fun.

indulge

Choose such pleasures as recreate much and cost little.

Richard Fuller

>> Splurge on a frugal indulgence. Give yourself small rewards as incentives to achieve a goal or finish a job.

#98

Create Mental Energy

Each of us makes our own weather, determines the color of the skies in the emotional universe which he inhabits.

Fulton J. Sheen

energy

You can create mental energy or drain it away. Tension, poor eating habits, lack of exercise, and negative thoughts can create a foul mood that steals your energy and leaves you feeling numb and depleted. Take care of your body. Exercise releases tension and gets your metabolism revved up. Good nutrition helps balance brain chemistry and gives you energy for life. New ideas stimulate your mind. Commit to lifelong learning and personal growth.

Overcome worry through affirmations and prayer. Cultivate an attitude of faith and hope. Trust in God connects you to resources of spirit, helping you tap into higher wisdom and insight.

>> Take a half-hour to walk or run. Regular rhythmic exercise like walking or running trains your body and helps you achieve mental clarity.

#99

Cultivate Inner Peace

A mind occupied with fear is a great obstacle standing between you and the abundant life you were created for. Ease the stress of fear by learning to cultivate inner peace. By cultivating inner peace, you become more receptive to the grace of God, more able to rest and trust in his love.

Begin by noticing the small fears that control you—fear of failing, or fears of being criticized or rejected. Now consciously take those fears and offer them to God. Focus your mind on God instead of your fears. Visualize those fears dissolving in the light of God's love. Rest in God's peace.

peace

> *I'm leaving you well and whole. That's my parting gift to you. Peace. I don't leave you the way you're used to being left— feeling abandoned, bereft.*
>
> John 14:27
> THE MESSAGE

>> Make a list of the fears that are weighing on your mind. Write an affirmation or find a Bible promise for each one.

#100

Appreciate the Good

Is it so small a thing to have enjoyed the sun, to have lived light in the spring, to have loved, to have thought, to have done?

Matthew Arnold

appreciate

Life is a precious gift from God. Instead of being stressed over what you don't have, enjoy the gifts God has given you. Cherish your family and loved ones. They will not be here forever, and neither will you. Take time to see how beautiful and unique each person is and remember what each one means to you. Focus on the good and be patient with the less than perfect.

Enjoy the beauty of the earth. Appreciate the passing parade of life, reveling in the colors, sights, sounds, flavors, and textures of existence here on earth. Treasure sweet memories and make each moment memorable.

>> Tell someone how much you appreciate him or her. Write a love letter to God, thanking him for all the gifts he has given you.

#101

Trust in the Goodness of God

You have come this far by faith. Even in the darkest times, God has not let you down. Even when things did not work out as you had hoped, they still worked out. God has walked with you in sunshine and through the valley of the shadow. You can rest in his care right now, knowing that God is with you in times of stress and difficulty as well as in good times.

Claim Romans 8:28 for your own: "God causes everything to work together for the good of those who love God and are called according to his purpose for them" (NLT).

trust

> *The LORD God is a sun and shield; the LORD will give grace and glory; no good thing will He withhold from those who walk uprightly.*
>
> Psalm 84:11 NKJV

>> Write about a time when God helped you through a difficult situation and list the unexpected blessings that grew out of it.

Be still and cool in thy own mind and spirit.

George Fox

Relax and rest. God has showered
you with blessings.

Psalm 116:7 THE MESSAGE